This book belongs to

Wesley Scherr

The New KIDS
Book of

ANGeL ViSiTS

The New Kids Book of Angel Visits

Published by New Kids Media™ in association with Baker Book House Company, Grand Rapids, Michigan.

ISBN 0-8010-4434-0

Printed in the United States of America

1 2 3 4 — 02 01 00 99

The New KIDS Book of

ANGEL VISITS

Anne Adams

Illustrated by Marlene McAuley

Published in
association with

For my children
Michal and Alexandra Tyra

Dear Parents,

It's never too early to begin teaching the truths of the Bible to your children. The Junior Reference Series will help young children understand the meaning of major Bible passages and see God's daily involvement in the lives of his people. They will enjoy learning about Bible animals and how their personalities were used to explain how people sometimes behave. Our prayer is that this series will instill in your child a lifelong thirst for knowledge of the Bible and it's message of love.

The Publishers

Hagar's Angel

GENESIS 16:1-15; 21:8-19

Hagar ran away to the desert. She was scared, sad, and alone. Her mistress Sarah gave her to Abraham to be his second wife, and now she was pregnant. Sarah wanted her to have Abraham's child because she thought she couldn't have her own. So why was Sarah treating her badly now? Suddenly, an angel of the Lord appeared. "Hagar," he said, "Where are you going?" The angel told her to go back and obey Sarah. He said she would have a son named Ishmael.

Years later, Abraham sent Hagar and Ishmael into the desert. Hagar watched her son drink his last drop of water. She cried, thinking her son would

die. An angel called from heaven, "Do not fear!" Then, a well of water appeared out of nowhere!

Three Visitors

Genesis 18

A braham sat beside his tent. It was a hot day, but the branches of an oak tree offered some shade. He looked up to see three men. Quickly, he ran to them and bowed low. He knew one was the Lord, and the other two were angels. He led them to the shady tree, and he and Sarah prepared a meal for them. The Lord told Abraham he was leaving to destroy the wicked cities of Sodom and Gomorrah.

"Oh no," thought Abraham. "My nephew Lot lives there!" The angels walked toward Sodom, but the Lord stayed for a moment. Abraham's heart pounded as he asked, "Lord, if you find ten godly people there, will you still

destroy the cities?" The Lord assured
Abraham that for ten godly men, the
cities would be spared.

Two Angels

GENESIS 19:1-29

Lot was the only godly man who lived in Sodom. When the two angels left Abraham, they traveled to the city. It was dark by the time they arrived. Lot watched them approach, and he bowed as they came near. "Please my lords," he said, "spend the night at my house."

At dawn, the angels led Lot, his wife, and their daughters out of the city. "Escape for your life," one angel cried. "Run and don't look behind you!" Terrified, Lot and his family ran. Fire and brimstone fell from the sky and destroyed Sodom and Gomorrah. As Lot's wife turned to look behind, she

became a pillar of salt. Lot could not stop. He ran with his daughters until they reached a safe place.

The Burning Bush

Moses led his sheep to the wilderness beside Mount Horeb. He watched them graze when all at once he saw a burning bush. As Moses moved closer to get a better look, an angel of the Lord appeared to him within the flames of fire. "Moses!" God called from the bush. Moses caught his breath and trembled. "Here I am," he said in a small voice.

"I am the God of your father, the God of Abraham, Isaac, and Jacob," the Lord said. Moses hid his face, afraid to look at God. "I am sending you to Pharaoh to bring my people, the Israelites, out of Egypt." Moses didn't know why God chose him. He was

afraid, but he agreed to do everything
God asked him on that day.

Balaam's Donkey

Numbers 22:21-35

Balaam saddled his donkey. He was going to see the leader of Moab who asked him to curse the Israelites. God told Balaam not to do it, but he kept thinking about all the money he would get if he did. Balaam did not see the angel of the Lord standing in the road with a sword. His donkey did, and she ran into a field. The angel appeared again, and the donkey pressed into a wall. The third time the angel appeared, the donkey laid down, terrified.

When God opened Balaam's eyes, he saw the angel and he fell down. The angel said, "Your path is a reckless one. If your donkey hadn't turned away, I would have killed you, but spared her."

Then the angel told Balaam what to do on his journey.

A Message for Gideon

Judges 6:11-23

Gideon was threshing wheat when an angel of the Lord came. The angel said, "The Lord is with you, mighty warrior." Gideon was confused, "if the Lord is with us, why has all this happened to us?" Why, he wondered, did the Midianites keep attacking the Israelites? The angel told Gideon that the Lord would use him to defeat the Midianites.

"Give me a sign that it is really you talking to me, Lord," he said. He prepared an offering and placed it on a rock. The angel touched it with his staff, and fire flared from the rock and ate the offering. After the angel disappeared, Gideon knew he had seen an angel of

the Lord. He was afraid. The Lord
comforted him, "Peace! Do not be
afraid!"

Samson's Birth Foretold

Judges 13:6-21

Manoah's wife ran to find him. "A man of God came to me," she told him excitedly. "He was awesome, like an angel. He told me I'd have a son, a Nazirite." Manoah dropped to his knees and prayed. The next day Manoah's wife was in the field when the angel visited again. She ran to get her husband.

Manoah asked him his name. "It is beyond understanding," the angel replied. Manoah prepared a burnt offering to the Lord and as the fire burned, the angel rose to heaven in the flame. Manoah was frightened. He and his wife fell with their faces to the ground. They knew the man was an angel of the Lord. Not long after,

Manoah's wife gave birth to a son, and he was called Samson.

Touched by an Ange

1 KINGS 19:1-8

Elijah was depressed. He had just run all the way from Mount Carmel where he had made short work of all the false prophets. Now he found out that Queen Jezebel wanted to kill him for what he had done. He was scared to death. He had to run. Elijah ran all day through the desert, then stopped to rest beneath a broom tree. "Lord, take my life," he prayed before he fell asleep.

At once, an angel touched him. "Get up and eat." He awoke to find bread and a jar of water. He ate and drank and fell back to sleep. Again, an angel touched him. "Get up and eat, for the journey ahead is too much for you." Elijah rose and ate. Then he traveled

forty days and forty nights to reach
Mount Horeb, the mountain of God.

The Fiery Furnace

Daniel 3:1-28

King Nebuchadnezzar looked at the statue of gold and was pleased. He didn't believe in God. He thought that all of the people in Babylon should worship the statue. Whoever didn't would be thrown into a hot furnace. When the king found out that Shadrach, Meshach, and Abednego refused to worship the statue, he was furious. "Throw them into the furnace," he ordered.

When the king looked inside he shouted, "Look! I see four men walking in the fire. They're not harmed and the fourth man looks like a son of the gods." When the men walked out of the furnace safely, the king was deeply moved.

"Praise be to God who sent his angel to
rescue his servants!" he cried.

The Den of Lions

Daniel just heard the news. A law was passed in Babylon which said that anyone who prayed to God would be thrown into a den of lions. With a heavy heart, he walked home and went to his upstairs room. Here the windows opened towards Jerusalem. He got down on his knees. Three times a day he prayed and gave thanks to God, just as he had done before.

When it was known that Daniel had prayed, he was captured and thrown into the den of lions. At the first light of dawn, Daniel heard the king shout, "Has your God been able to rescue you?"

Daniel called out, "My God sent his angel, and he shut the mouths of the

lions!" Daniel gave thanks to God as he
was lifted out of the den unharmed.

Gabriel visits Mary

Luke 1:26-38

Mary was engaged to be married to Joseph, and she looked forward to their life together. While she lived in Nazareth, the angel Gabriel appeared to her. "Greetings, you who are highly favored! The Lord is with you." Mary was troubled. What did this angel mean, she wondered.

Gabriel said, "Don't be afraid, Mary. You have found favor with God." The angel told her she would give birth to a son named Jesus. "He will be great and will be called the son of the Most High." Mary couldn't believe that God had chosen her. She was so proud. "I am the Lord's servant," she murmured. "May it be as you have said." When the

angel left Mary's thoughts were filled
with his words.

Joseph's Dream

Matthew 1:18-25

While Joseph was engaged to Mary, he learned that she was pregnant. He felt betrayed, and decided not to marry her. Joseph still loved Mary, and he didn't want her to be disgraced. He would break off their engagement quietly. One night while he was sleeping, an angel of the Lord appeared to him in a dream.

"Joseph, son of David," the angel said, "don't be afraid to take Mary as your wife. The baby in her womb is from the Holy Spirit. She'll have a son named Jesus and he will save people from their sins." When Joseph woke up, he knew he had to do what the angel of

the Lord said. He made Mary his wife.
Not long after, she gave birth to a son,
and they named him Jesus.

A Ladder to Heaven

Genesis 28:10-17

Jacob left his home to look for a wife. He traveled for a day and stopped when the sun set. He found a large stone, laid it under his head and fell asleep. Then he had an amazing dream. In his dream, he saw a ladder that reached up through the stars into heaven. The angels of God moved up and down the ladder. They traveled from heaven to earth, running errands for God.

The Lord stood above the ladder and said, "I am the Lord, the God of Abraham and Isaac. I will give you and your descendants the land upon which you are lying." Jacob woke up afraid. He looked around and whispered, "This is

an awesome place! It must be the house
of God, the gate of heaven."

Jacob Wrestles an Angel

GENESIS 32:24-30

Jacob was alone in the dark when an angel of the Lord came and wrestled with him. They fought the whole night. Jacob used all his might, and the angel couldn't overpower him. Then the angel touched his hip, and it came loose in its socket. Though Jacob couldn't wrestle anymore, he held on tight. As the sun rose, the angel said, "Let me go, for it is daybreak."

Jacob held on. "I won't let you go until you bless me," he said. The angel told him, "Your name will no longer be Jacob. You will be called Israel because you have struggled with God and men and you have overcome." The angel blessed him, and Jacob was

relieved. He had seen God's face and
lived.

The Temptation of Jesu

Matthew 4:1-11

The Spirit led Jesus into the desert. He was going to be tempted by the devil. After fasting for forty days and nights, he was very hungry. The devil whispered, "If you're the son of God, tell these stones to become bread." Jesus refused. The devil took him to the top of the temple and told him to jump so the angels could save him. Jesus refused.

Finally, the devil brought him to a very high mountain and showed him the kingdoms and riches of the world. "All this I will give you if you bow down and worship me," he said. Jesus replied, "Away from me Satan! For it is written: 'Worship the Lord your God, and serve

him only.'" The devil left, and angels came and took care of Jesus.

Shepherds in the Field

Luke 2:8-15

Shepherds lived in the fields near Bethlehem. Lovingly, they tended their flocks by day and watched over them at night. One night an angel of the Lord appeared to some of them and the glory of the Lord shone around them. The shepherds were terrified. "Don't be afraid," the angel told them. "I bring you good news. Today, a Savior has been born to you. He is Christ the Lord."

The shepherds watched in amazement as more angels filled the night sky. Together, they raised their sweet voices praising God and singing, "Glory to God in the highest, and on earth peace to men!" Then as suddenly

as the angels appeared, they returned to heaven. The shepherds were filled with awe.

Zechariah's Promise

Luke 1:8-23

While Zechariah was in the temple burning incense to the Lord, an angel appeared by the altar. Zechariah shook with fright, but the angel said, "Do not be afraid. Your prayer has been heard. Your wife Elizabeth will have a son, and he will be great in the sight of the Lord."

Zechariah wasn't sure he believed the angel. "How can I be sure of this?" he asked. The angel replied, "I am Gabriel. I stand in the presence of God. I've been sent to speak to you and tell you this good news." Gabriel told him that because of his disbelief, he would lose his voice for a time. Zechariah left the temple unable to speak. His voice

returned when his wife gave birth to
their son, John the Baptist.

An Angel for Jesus

Luke 22:39-45

Jesus left Jerusalem and walked to the Mount of Olives where it was quiet and peaceful. Here he could be alone with God and not be disturbed by the crowds of the city. The disciples followed him, and he told them to pray. Then he walked a short distance from them and knelt down. "Father," he prayed in anguish, "if you are willing, take this cup from me; yet not my will, but yours be done." Jesus knew he would be crucified soon. He dreaded the times ahead, but wanted to do God's will.

An angel from heaven appeared to Jesus and strengthened him. He prayed even more and felt beads of sweat roll

from his body like blood trickling to the ground. He got up and returned to the disciples.

An Angel at the Tomb

Matthew 28:1-7

It was still dark that morning when Mary Magdalene and her friend went to visit the tomb where Jesus was buried. All at once the earth shook, and an angel of the Lord came to the tomb. He rolled away the stone which sealed the entrance. He looked like lightning and his clothes were white like snow.

The soldiers who guarded the tomb shivered. Mary and her friend stood frozen in fear. Gently, the angel spoke, "Don't be afraid. I know you are looking for Jesus who was crucified. He's not here: he has risen, just as he said." Mary looked inside the tomb. Only the cloths which wrapped Jesus' body were left.

"Go quickly," said the angel, "and tell his disciples the good news."

Jesus Ascends to Heaven

Acts 1:9-11

The eleven disciples gathered by Jesus on the Mount of Olives. They sensed something was about to happen. They watched Jesus as he lifted up his hands and blessed them. Then, while he was blessing them, he rose to heaven and a cloud hid him from view. The disciples stood and stared into the sky as he was rising. All at once, two angels dressed in white, stood beside them.

"Men of Galilee," they said, "why do you stand looking into the sky? The same Jesus who was taken from you into heaven, will return in the same way he left." The disciples loved Jesus and were sad to see him go. They bowed down to worship him, and by the time they

returned to Jerusalem, they were filled
with joy because of the angels' promise.

Jail Doors Open

Acts 5:12-21

Peter joined the apostles near the temple. Crowds of people pushed against one another waiting to be touched by God. "Praise the Lord!" he rejoiced when those who passed within his shadow were healed by God's power. All at once, soldiers grabbed him from behind. He and the other apostles were arrested, jailed, and beaten.

That night, Peter and the others sat huddled in their cramped cell. They stared with wide eyes as an angel of the Lord appeared and opened the jail doors. "Go to the temple courts," he told them. "Tell people the full message of this new life." Quietly, the apostles slipped past the guards. They entered the temple area

at daybreak and began to teach the
people just as the angel had instructed
them.

An Angel Directs Philip

Philip was amazed. The people in Samaria were hungry to hear God's word. When he preached, crowds pressed close to him. Evil spirits flew from people, and cripples got up and walked! Then one day Philip heard an angel of the Lord say to him, "Go south and follow the desert road." Philip didn't hesitate. He left right away.

While he walked the dusty path, he saw an important man from Ethiopia sitting in his chariot reading the book of Isaiah. Philip heard the Spirit say, "Go to that chariot and stay near it." He got in and told the man about Jesus. Now he knew why the angel sent him here! After

he baptized the man in water, the Spirit
of the Lord suddenly took Philip away to
another city.

Cornelius

Acts 10:1-8

Cornelius was a Roman officer in the Italian Regiment. He was a centurion in charge of 100 soldiers. He loved God and helping those in need. One afternoon he had a vision. An angel of the Lord called, "Cornelius!" He trembled in fear. "What is it Lord?" he whispered.

The angel replied, "Your prayers have been heard by God. Your gifts to the poor have been noticed. Now, send men to Joppa to bring back a man named Simon who is also called Peter. He is staying with Simon the tanner, whose house is by the sea." As soon as the angel left, Cornelius sent two of his

servants and a soldier. "Quick!" he told
them. "Go to Joppa and find this man
called Peter."

Peter Escapes

Acts 12:5-11

The angel of the Lord glided past sentries guarding the prison entrance. When he entered the dark cell, his light shone on the prisoner. Peter was chained between two soldiers. He struck Peter on the side. "Quick! Get up!" The chains fell from Peter's wrists. "Put on your clothes and sandals," he urged. "Wrap your cloak around you and follow me."

Peter left the prison dreamily. The angel knew Peter thought he was just seeing a vision. He led him past the first and second guards and to the iron gate leading to the city. It opened by itself, and they walked through. The angel's

mission was over. As he left, he heard
Peter say, "Lord! You sent your angel
and rescued me!"

A Storm at Sea

Acts 27:9-44

Paul stood on the deck of the ship and watched the storm clouds. He tried to warn the crew not to sail, but no one listened. Before long the wind and waves battered the ship until finally the sailors gave up and were driven along. Paul knew the sailors had lost all hope of being saved.

Then during the cold night, Paul felt the warmth of an angel. "Don't be afraid, Paul," he said, "you must stand trial before Caesar. God has graciously given you the lives of all who sail with you." The next day Paul told the men about the angel's visit. "Keep up your courage, men. I have faith that it will

happen as God told me." Weeks after
they set sail, the ship landed safely on
the island of Malta.

Gabriel Visits Danie

DaNieL 8:15-27; 9:20-23

Daniel tried to understand the vision
God gave him, but it wasn't easy.
He saw a man approaching, and he
heard a voice call out, "Gabriel, tell this
man the meaning of the vision." Daniel
was terrified, and he fell to the ground in
a deep sleep. Gabriel touched him,
raised him to his feet, and explained the
meaning of the vision. After Gabriel left,
Daniel was exhausted for several days.

Sometime later while Daniel was
praying, Gabriel flew swiftly to him.
"Daniel," he said, "I have come to give
you insight and understanding. As soon
as you prayed, an answer was given. I
have come to tell you, for you are highly

esteemed." Daniel listened while Gabriel
explained the meaning of the vision.

Pharaoh and the Israelites

EXODUS 14

Moses and the Israelites were camped near the Red Sea when they heard the sound of chariots. Pharaoh's army raced toward them armed with swords and spears. The Israelites cried to Moses, "What have you done to us bringing us out of Egypt?" Moses raised his voice above their screams. "Do not be afraid. Stand firm and you will see the deliverance the Lord will bring you today."

As they waited, an angel of the Lord who was traveling in front of them moved behind them. A pillar of cloud also moved to the back. The Israelites knew they were safely separated from Pharaoh's army. Moses stretched out his

hand over the sea, and the Lord drove
the water back with a strong wind so
they could escape.

A Heavenly Army

2 KINGS 6:8-17

Early one morning, Elisha's servant went outside. An army of war horses and chariots were spread over the hill like a swarm of locusts ready to fly. He ran inside to find Elisha. "Oh, my Lord," he cried in fear. "What shall we do?" Elisha tried to calm him. "Don't be afraid. Those who are with us are more than those who are with them." The servant looked at Elisha in confusion. "Has he gone mad?" he thought. "There is two of us and thousands of them."

Elisha prayed that the eyes of his servant would be opened. When they stepped outside, the servant was surprised to see a huge heavenly army.

The hills were filled with God's horses,
and Elisha was surrounded by chariots
of fire and an army of angels.

Abraham is Tested

GENESIS 22:1-18

"Abraham!" God called. "Take your only son, Isaac, whom you love. Go to the region of Moriah. Sacrifice him there as a burnt offering." Abraham's heart was heavy. He didn't understand, but he knew God had a reason for asking him to do this. The next morning he took Isaac to the place God told him about.

Abraham tied up Isaac and laid him on the altar. Tears filled his eyes as he held the knife above him. Then an angel of the Lord said, "Abraham! Don't lay a hand on the boy. I know you fear God because you have not withheld from me your only son. Because you

have done this, I will surely bless you."
Abraham untied Isaac. He held him
close and gave thanks to God.

A Mighty Ange

JOSHUA 5:13-15, 6:1-5

Joshua was near Jericho when he glanced up and saw a man standing in front of him. He was holding a sword. "Are you for us or for our enemies?" Joshua asked.

"Neither," the man replied, "but as commander of the army of the Lord I have now come!" Joshua realized the man was an angel. He was so mighty, he was in charge of all of God's army!

Joshua fell to the ground. "What message does the Lord have for his servant?" he asked.

The angel replied, "Take off your sandals, for the place where you are standing is holy."

Then the Lord said, "I have delivered Jericho into your hands along with its king and its fighting men." He told Joshua exactly what he needed to do in order to capture the city.

Jacob's Dream

GENESIS 31:1-21

Jacob noticed that Laban, his father-in-law, wasn't treating him the same anymore. He wasn't as nice as he used to be. He said to his wives, Leah and Rachel, "I've worked for your father with all my strength. Yet he's cheated me by changing my wages ten times."

Then the angel of God called to him in a dream, "Jacob!"

He answered, "Here I am!"

The angel told him, "I've seen what Laban has done to you. I am the God of Bethel where you annointed a pillar and where you made a vow to me. Now leave this place at once and go back to your native land." Jacob put his children and wives on camels and drove

his livestock ahead. He was glad to
return to the land of Canaan.

Zechariah's Vision

Zechariah 1:8-13

During the night, Zechariah had a vision. He saw an angel riding a red horse. He was standing among the myrtle trees in a ravine. Behind him were red, brown, and white horses. Zechariah was curious. "What are these my Lord?" he asked. The angel explained, "They are the ones the Lord has sent to go throughout the earth."

Then the horses spoke to the angel, "We have gone throughout the earth and found the whole world at rest and in peace."

The angel said, "Lord Almighty, how long will you withhold mercy from Jerusalem and the towns of Judah which you have been angry with?" The Lord

answered the angel's question with kind
and comforting words.

David's Choice

2 Sam. 24:11-17, 1 Chron. 21:11,12

When David sinned against God, the Lord told him to choose his punishment. He could run from his enemies for three years, Israel could suffer three years of famine, or Israel could endure three days of a plague while an angel destroyed the land. David was upset, "What a choice!" he thought.

He finally decided that it was better to fall into the Lord's hands and pray for mercy than to fall into enemy hands. God sent a plague on Israel and seventy-thousand people died. When the angel of the Lord stretched out his hand to destroy Jerusalem, the Lord was grieved because of all the suffering. "Enough!" he commanded the angel,

"withdraw your hand." David knew that
God would have mercy when men
would not.

Angels in Heaven

Revelation 4:1-6; 5:11-14

God opened John's eyes and allowed him to see a door standing open in heaven. He called to him, like a trumpet, "Come up here!" At once John was standing in the throne room where God was seated. He didn't know where to look first. What looked like a sea of glass, clear as crystal, was in front of the throne. Thousands of angels were circling. They sang, "Worthy is the Lamb who was slain, to receive power and wealth and wisdom and strength and honor and glory and praise!"

Then John heard every creature in heaven and on earth, under the earth, and in the sea singing: "To him who sits

on the throne and to the Lamb be praise
and honor and glory and power, for ever
and ever!"

Angels meet Jacob

GENESIS 32:1-2

Jacob was stressed. First he ran away from Laban, his father-in-law, because he wasn't treating him right. When Laban came after him Jacob was afraid. He knew it was God's grace that kept Laban from hurting him. Now Jacob was leaving to find his brother Esau. He hadn't seen him for years. Laban hadn't killed him, but Esau might. Jacob had stolen his birthright years ago!

On his way, the angels of God met him. He recognized them at once by their appearance. "This is surely the camp of God!" he said out loud. He gave the place a special name. Jacob knew that God was with him. He was not

alone. He had nothing to fear so he went
on his way in peace.

The Passover

EXodUS 12

After Pharaoh refused to set the Israelites free from slavery, Moses knew God was going to bring the final plague on Egypt. He gathered the leaders of Israel and told them, "Take some lamb's blood and smear it on the top and sides of the doorframe. Not one of you shall leave your house until morning."

At midnight, the angel of death went through the land. He passed by every Israelite door which had blood on it. In the Egyptian homes he killed every firstborn creature, people and animals. As Moses sat in his home, he listened to the wailing and sobs of the Egyptians.

"If only Pharaoh had listened to the word of God," he thought sadly.

An Angel at the Poo

Jesus walked under the covered porches at the Pool of Bethesda. He stepped around the people laying on mats. Some were blind, others couldn't walk. He knew they came here often. They waited for an angel to come and stir up the water. The first one to step into the pool after it was stirred, was healed.

Jesus met a man at the pool who had been sick for thirty-eight years. He was filled with compassion for him. "Do you want to get well?" Jesus asked.

"Sir," the sick man replied, "I have no one to help me into the pool when the water is stirred. When I try to climb in, someone else goes first."

Jesus was touched by his words.
"Get up!" He said. "Pick up your mat
and walk!" At once, the man was cured.

Herod Dies

Acts 12:19-23

King Herod's life was filled with problems. Recently, he threw Peter in prison only to find out he had escaped. Now he had to deal with the people in Tyre and Sidon. He was tired of quarreling with them. When he found out they wanted to meet with him and make peace he thought, "Ha! They've finally realized they need me to survive!"

He dressed in his royal robes and sat on the throne. As he addressed the people, they began to shout, "This is the voice of a god, not a man." Herod was delighted. "I deserve this praise as much as any god," he thought smugly. God did

not agree. All at once an angel of the
Lord struck him down. Not long after,
Herod died a terrible death.

God's Throne Room

Isaiah 6:1-7

Isaiah saw the Lord seated on a throne. The train of his robe filled the temple and angels flew above him. Each angel had six wings. Two wings covered their faces, two covered their feet, and two were used for flight. He heard them call to one another, "Holy, holy, holy is the Lord Almighty. The whole earth is full of his glory."

At the sound of their voices the doors shook, and the temple filled with smoke. Isaiah was afraid. "Woe to me!" he cried. "I am ruined! I'm a sinner and my eyes have seen the Lord."

One of the angels plucked a live coal from the altar with tongs. He flew to Isaiah and touched the coal to his

mouth. "See," the angel said, "now your
guilt is taken away and your sin is
forgiven."

Four Corners

Revelation 7:1-12

John saw four angels standing at the four corners of the earth. They gripped the four winds tightly to keep the wind from blowing on the land, the sea, or on any tree. He saw another angel moving up from the east. He was holding the seal of the living God. He heard this angel call to the others, "Do not harm the land or the sea or the trees until we put a seal on the foreheads of the servants of our God."

Then John watched all the angels gather around the throne. They fell down, their faces before the throne. They worshiped God, saying, "Amen! Praise and glory and wisdom

and thanks and honor and power and
strength be to our God for ever and ever.
Amen!"

Other books in this series include:

The New Kids Book of Bible People

The New Kids Book of Bible Animals

The New Kids Book of Bible Passages